Contents

KW-223-043

The miracle of the *Oceanos*

There is an enduring seafaring custom known as the Birkenhead Drill – "women and children first" – in honour of the British troop carrier *HMS Birkenhead* which hit a reef in 1852. Fearing that the life-boats carrying women and children would be swamped, the commanding officer asked his men to "Stand fast!" Not a man moved – 445 of them went down with the ship.

But on the evening of Saturday, August 3, 1991, when the passenger liner *Oceanos* set sail on her fateful voyage from the Buffalo River harbour in South Africa, not one of the ship's senior officers was to honour the Birkenhead Drill.

The *Oceanos* was a giant of a ship: 150 metres long, six decks tall, weighing 12,000 tonnes. She was 39 years old, no longer in the prime of life, but she was luxuriously appointed and carried the highest possible safety rating from Lloyd's Register of Shipping.

There were 571 people on board when *Oceanos* nosed her way out of the harbour entrance to head north towards Durban, some 435 kilometres up the treacherous east coast of Africa. There were 361 passengers, and 184 crew members, 6 administrators and, finally, 20 ship's entertainers, employed to organize the social whirl which passengers expected on their fair-weather holiday cruises.

"The passengers are on holiday," cruise director Lorraine Betts told her team of administrators and entertainers. "You're here to work." The group smiled back at her grimly; they had entertained a large wedding party in harbour the previous day and had only managed to catnap during the past 48 hours. Now, without pause, the revelry was due to start all over again.

It was 8pm that night when the *Oceanos* began to pitch and roll in the huge waves whipped up by a 40-knot wind. Below decks, passengers playing slot machines in the ship's casino were thrown across the room as the deck slipped away from under their feet. From the next door lounge there was a cry of "Watch out!" as the grand piano crashed from the stage.

"I think we're in for a rough time," one passenger remembers saying to his wife.

A ship's musician, Tracy Hill, was dozing fitfully in her cabin, catching up on lost sleep. Suddenly, an ear-splitting crash woke her. Heavy cabin trunks had been tossed across the room and smashed against the wall. There was a dense curtain of white foam boiling at the closed porthole; suddenly, water spurted through the seal, soaking everything in the cabin.

Outside the door, her husband, Moss, was about to put his key in the lock when three agitated ship's security officers staggered past him along the passageway. Curious, he followed. Outside a door marked "Generator Room", oil-smeared crew members were dripping water all over the floor, yelling at each other at the tops of their voices.

Then the entire ship was plunged into total darkness as a dull explosion sent a tremor through the vessel. The *Oceanos* lay dead in the water, rolling and slewing sideways in the enormous swells. The emergency generator cut in, throwing eerie, half-light shadows everywhere.

The deck officers were huddled on the bridge, white-faced. Captain Yiannis Avranas, still dressed in his tropical whites, looked stunned, haggard, no longer the cool and dashing figure he had cut earlier in the day. His officers were staring at him in nervous silence. The staff captain was shouting over and over again into the radio: "Mayday... Mayday... Mayday..."

The door to the bridge burst open, bringing with it the howling sounds of a raging gale. The chief engineer staggered in, stuttering with shock and fear, already wearing a life-jacket and clutching a duffel bag to his chest. "H-h-h-hull plates have fractured on the starboard side," he stammered breathlessly. "The watertight doors won't stop the flooding."

"Oh, my God," muttered Avranas. In stunned silence he struggled to come to terms with the fact that there was nothing to stop the sea pouring through the web of drainage pipes, surging from outlets all over the ship, gradually flooding the vessel deck by deck. In no time at all the build up of water in the bows would drag her down.

"How fast is the water coming in?" he barked.

"We only have a few hours." The chief engineer swung on his heels and raced off the bridge.

"The crew knows we're sinking," reported a breathless deck officer. "They're abandoning ship."

Bewildered, Avranas looked around him. Officers who had been standing on the bridge only minutes before had already slipped away. The captain shrugged and hurried to his cabin. "Get dressed," he told his wife and their four-year-old daughter. "We're in trouble."

One of the ship's magicians, Robin Boltman, was on his way to the main lounge when members of the crew rushed past him. He tumbled after them up on to the lifeboat deck, and his jaw dropped at what he saw. A jostling, screaming crowd of fully-dressed officers and crew were piling into a lifeboat.

Back in the lounge he relayed the news to Lorraine Betts. "Let them go, we don't need scared people around," she declared. Then she hurried off to confront the captain.

"What's happening?" she demanded. Avranas would not meet her eyes. "How serious is the situation, Captain?" she asked firmly.

"Everyone must gather in the main lounge. Tell your staff to fetch life-jackets from below," he answered.

Lorraine hurried below. Can he handle the situation? she wondered. He already seems a bundle of nerves. Don't say he's buckling under the strain.

She mustered her staff – singers, dancers, musicians, cabaret artistes and hostesses. "Quiet!" she ordered the chattering, nervous group. "The captain says we have engine trouble. There's been some flooding below. Nothing serious. Go to each cabin and tell everyone to assemble for lifeboat drill in the main lounge. No passengers are allowed back below. Bring all the life-jackets and blankets you can find. No questions!" she declared as a babble of voices broke out around her. "Just do as I say."

Soon, hundreds of passengers, many in jeans and T-shirts, others in suits and cocktail dresses, a handful dressed only in flimsy night clothes, were sitting in the gloomy lounge. Robin Boltman, the magician, was climbing on to the stage.

"Sorry about the lights, folks. We forgot to pay the bill," he joked. "May I have your attention, please."

The passengers stirred. John and Gail Adamson, who had taken the trip to celebrate their eleventh wedding anniversary, squatted on the floor, tying on their children's life-jackets with trembling fingers. Only 17 days before, Gail had given birth to a son; the baby, together with his two sisters, aged eight and two, were on board with them. John looked at his wife. Whatever's gone wrong, it can't be all that bad, he told himself. Passenger liners don't sink, not in this day and age.

A hostess leaned over John's shoulder. "Take your wife and children into the foyer," she suggested quietly. Gail swaddled a blanket around baby John and clutched him against her life-jacket. John swept pyjama-clad Kari into the air and struggled out of the lounge with eight-year-old Samantha's arms wrapped firmly around his legs. Outside, on the windswept promenade deck, John could sense, rather than see, the awesome power of the sea. The wind lashed his face with spume; it felt like the sting of a whip.

A steward eased baby John out of Gail's arms and helped her to half-crawl, half-walk through the mass of struggling bodies; she turned as John called, "Here, take Kari and Samantha." He thrust the children towards her.

A lifeboat was already dangling over the side, swinging wildly above the seething waves. Lorraine Betts, together with guitarist Moss Hills, and his magician friend Julian Butler, were forming the passengers into a straggling, staggering queue.

Captain Avranas was there, shepherding his wife and daughter into the lifeboat. He turned, "Lorraine, I must get help," he shouted, and then started to scramble into the tiny, already overcrowded boat. An arm reached out for his life-jacket and pulled him roughly back to the deck.

Baby John, then Kari and Samantha, were lifted into the lifeboat. Gail prepared to say goodbye to them, perhaps for ever. Please, God, look after them, she silently prayed. Lorraine slapped her on the shoulder. Gail looked around. "Go!" ordered Lorraine. With a sob of relief, Gail jumped into the boat to join her children.

"Lower away!" Lorraine shouted. The boat fell into the night, lurching and crashing against the side of the ship before hitting the water with a spine-shattering thump.

Mothers and children were tossed like rag dolls from their seats. Looking over the side from the promenade deck, Lorraine watched the boat swoop and corkscrew on the giant black waves. She heard the engine fire, crest a wave, and disappear into the blackness.

In the distance, plunging through the mountainous seas, she could see the lights of approaching ships. Rescue teams all along the coast, alerted by the rescue co-ordination centre in Cape Town, had swung into action.

In the lounge of the *Oceanos,* a crowd of young men was singing rugby songs. A solitary woman was crying, "I can't swim," she sobbed. Moss and Tracy Hill grabbed their guitars and jumped on to the stage. Soon everybody was singing.

Someone tapped John Adamson on the shoulder. "We need strong men to row the next lifeboat," said a voice in his ear. He crawled out of the lounge, no longer able to stand upright on the sloping, rolling deck, to where Lorraine Betts half-pushed him on to the waiting lifeboat. Looking back, he saw Captain Avranas struggling to reach the lifeboat, and someone pulling him away.

Slowly, painfully slowly, the passengers were shepherded in groups from the lounge to their lifeboat stations. Patiently, Lorraine Betts and Robin Boltman filled the boats before watching them slip away into the darkness. There were eight lifeboats on the *Oceanos*, enough for everybody on board. But only five had been got away.

"Help me count how many passengers are still in the lounge," Lorraine told her staff. They found there were still more than 250 people on board. In the dining room, just two decks down from the lounge, chairs were already floating as the sea began to sweep through the *Oceanos*.

"Move everybody up to the upper deck," she ordered. "When the ship starts to down, we'll line up at the rails and jump into the sea. Meantime, someone must go up on the bridge to keep watch." It was 3am when the remaining passengers began to inch their way out of the lounge on to the open deck, clinging to each other for support, bruising themselves as the ship rolled and they were flung against the bulkheads.

When the rescue helicopter pilot Chaz Goatley flew over the *Oceanos*, the ship's vast white hull was already wallowing ponderously, her rails awash, her stern beginning to lift clear of the water, her bows nose-diving into the sea. Hundreds of people, all in orange life-jackets, were lining the steeply heeling deck.

The helicopter hovered over the vessel, carrying two navy divers harnessed to a wire from the belly of the chopper. One, Paul Whiley, was dropped on to the stern and the other, Gary Scoular, was lowered into the bows. The passengers began to cheer.

Moss Hill slithered down the steeply sloping deck to greet diver Scoular. "I'm the ship's guitarist," he said.

"You can help me put people in the harness," said Scoular. "Where's the crew?"

Moss grimaced. "Gone in the boats."

"Nice one," said Scoular, bitterly.

In the stern section, Whiley shouted at a queue of passengers waiting to be rescued. "We'll hoist two people at a time." He could only just be heard over the constant howl of the wind and the clatter of the helicopter rotor blades.

"OK, who's first?"

Captain Avranas thrust his way past a line of young women, ignoring the tears running down their cheeks. He quickly buckled himself into one of the harnesses. Whiley gave the badges of rank on his shoulders a long, hard stare, then shrugged and let him go.

The line jerked and the captain became the first person to be air-lifted off the sinking deck of the *Oceanos,* open-mouthed passengers staring up at him in disbelief.

When the empty wire was returned from the chopper to the deck, the ship's radio officer was the next to force his way to the front of the queue, followed by the ship's purser and a deck-hand. Whiley hadn't time to argue with them. Seven people were carried on the first helicopter: the captain, two officers, a sailor, and three women. 243 people were still left on board.

One by one, with dawn breaking and the *Oceanos* all the time settling lower and lower into the water, the liner's passengers were winched to safety. But in the forward part of the ship, naval diver Gary Scoular detected a gradual but dramatic change in the way the vessel was lying in the water. He realized some way had to be found to speed up the evacuation.

He had spotted some tiny motor launches, used by passengers to potter around the smooth waters of their harbour stop-overs, stacked in the bow. He slithered down the steepening slope of the deck towards the very front of the ship.

Waves were crashing over the bows and loose oil drums were rolling across the deck. Then, as if by magic, a Filipino crewman mysteriously appeared at Scoular's side. Together they manhandled a launch into the sea. Scoular dived after it and hauled himself on board. The engine started first time. He yelled to Lorraine Betts and Julian Butler at the rail of the liner: "Bring people!"

One by one, passengers flung themselves into the sea and swam to the launch. A non-swimmer hesitated at the rail of the ship. Butler grabbed his life-jacket and dragged the man overboard with him. Scoular and Butler made six trips from the *Oceanos* to ships' lifeboats standing off from rescuing vessels. They saved about 40 people.

On the final trip Scoular shouted to Lorraine, "Come on!"

"Wait!" she yelled back, making her way to the bridge. She counted the heads of passengers still awaiting rescue.

There were only a few, waiting patiently at the stern air-lift point. "Moss," she called, "I've been ordered off." Moss Hill gave a weary wave. Lorraine jumped into the sea. When she clawed her way over the side into the launch her watch had stopped at 10.20am.

From the window of the radio room on the bridge, Robin Boltman gave a thumbs up to Moss Hill. Moss was helping his wife Tracy push people up the deck to the air-lift point where two passengers, Piet Niemand and his grown-up son Peter, had taken over at the stern section harness. "Let go of the rails and raise your arms," Piet told people as they slipped the harness under their armpits and drew the buckles tight. Then he and his son gave a thumbs up: "Go!"

When only a handful of people were left on the stern, Piet urged his son to be winched to safety. The young man refused to leave. Piet reached down and gently helped an elderly woman, who had somehow been overlooked, to her feet. She could barely stand. "Son, take this lady up with you, as a favour to me."

It was a request Peter couldn't refuse. "Hold me as tight as you can," he smiled at the shivering woman. She wrapped her thin arms around him. Piet craned his neck so that he could watch his son and the frail burden clutched to him being winched to the safety of the helicopter.

Eventually, only Niemand, Whiley, Moss, Tracy and the mysterious Filipino seaman were left on the deck. The unidentified seaman, the only member of the liner's crew to stay with the ship until the end, read Psalm 23; "Yea, though I walk through the valley of the shadow of death, I will fear no evil; for thou art with me..."

Looking down from the bridge, Robin Boltman signed off over the radio: "*Oceanos* is about to go down. I'm leaving the bridge." He waved a salute down at Gary Scoular and Julian Butler who were standing off in the launch watching the ship go through her final death throes.

The naval diver Whiley and passenger Niemand were the last to be winched off the ship to a hovering helicopter.

The *Oceanos* toppled over and took her final plunge to the grave at 1.46pm, August 4, 1991. Every one of the 571 people on board were saved. That was the miracle of the *Oceanos*.

Lorraine Betts, Moss and Tracy Hill, Julian Butler, Robin Boltman and Piet Niemand were awarded the Wolraad medal, South Africa's highest award for civilian valour.

Helicopter pilot Chaz Goatley, and naval divers Gary Scoular and Paul Whiley were decorated by the South African Defence Force.

The Greek Maritime Board found Captain Yiannis Avranas and five of his senior officers guilty of negligence and of abandoning their passengers.

Lightning

Lightning is one of the most spectacular sights of nature. Sheet lightning occurs within a cloud. Forked lightning follows a zig-zag path from a cloud to the ground, or from one cloud to another.

Lightning is simply a gigantic spark of static electricity. Electricity does not normally flow through the air. It requires an electrical "pressure" of 10,000 volts to send a spark of electricity across an air gap of one centimetre. More than 1,000,000 volts would be needed to create a flash of lightning. Scientists believe that these great electrical charges are produced by friction between the ice crystals and water droplets in the turbulent air currents.

Thunder is the sound of air expanding as it is violently heated by the lightning. We see a flash of lightning before we hear the thunder because light travels much faster than sound. It is possible to tell how far away a storm is by counting the seconds between the flash of lightning and the sound of thunder. Sound takes about 3 seconds to travel through 1 km of air.

LUCKY ESCAPE

In Edinburgh one man had a lucky escape after lightning hit his umbrella.

Russell Dean, 30, a graphic designer, said: "There was a huge flash and my thumb was hit by what must have been the lightning. I jumped and the umbrella fell out of my hand. I kept the brolly down and just ran in the rain after that. I had heard that lightning doesn't strike twice but I didn't want to take any chances."

CHILDREN SURVIVE BOLT HITTING HOME

Two children escaped with barely a scratch when their home fell in around them after being struck by lightning.

Their mother could not believe they had survived the explosion which blew the roof off their two-storey home.

"When I heard their screams it was the best sound I have ever heard because it meant they were still alive," said Linda Milne yesterday.

Karen, seven, and Fraser, four, were in the lounge of their Aberdeenshire home when lightning struck the chimney stack. Granite blocks, roofing slates and mounds of lathing and plaster were hurled into the garden of the Sheiling, Tullynessle, by the force of the blast.

The strike came during a heavy rain storm and Mrs Milne was outside trying to stop flood water pouring into the property.

She had sent the children indoors for safety as she worked with her brother, Kenneth Watson, to divert the water from the cottage, near Alford.

"There was a huge bang and I felt as if I was being forced into the ground," said Mrs Milne.

"I looked up and saw my house was in total destruction.... I thought the children might have been killed," she added.

Earthquakes

Earthquakes are caused by movements which occur at the edges of the giant plates which make up the Earth's crust. These plates float on the hot, molten rock of the mantle below and are constantly on the move. As one plate slides past another, the rocks at the edges of the plates grind together. Sometimes the plates do not move smoothly and the two edges stick together until with a great jerk, they snap past each other. This sudden release of energy causes an earthquake. Shock waves, called seismic waves, spread outwards from the centre of the earthquake – called the epicentre. The deeper the epicentre, the further the shock waves travel, causing damage over a wide area.

Chile (1960)

Chile, in South America, experiences frequent earthquakes. In 1903, 3,000 people were killed and in 1939, 40,000 people died. The city of Concepcíon has been destroyed five times by earthquakes.

In June 1960 the most violent earthquake in modern times hit Chile, killing 5,700 people and making over 1 million people homeless. The earthquake's epicentre was at Concepcíon – it measured 8.5 on the Richter scale. The tremors, or earth movements, shook down buildings, trapping hundreds of people in the ruins. Huge cracks appeared in the ground. The earthquake triggered landslides and avalanches in the surrounding areas.

Armenia (1988)

On 7 December 1988, Armenia (at that time a republic of the former USSR) was struck by one of the strongest earthquakes ever recorded. Worst hit was the large town of Spitak, which was completely destroyed. It was estimated that over 55,000 people died during the disaster.

Armenia is a remote and underdeveloped country. Lack of equipment such as bulldozers and cranes made rescue attempts almost impossible.

500,000 people were made homeless – with only tents for shelter against the harsh winter weather. After their plight was reported on television and in newspapers around the world international relief workers began to arrive to help in the stricken area.

FAMOUS EARTHQUAKES

1201   Syria: possibly the earthquake which caused the largest loss of life in human history. An estimated 1 million people died.

1556   Shensi Province, China: an estimated 850,000 people died.

1896   Honshu, Japan: a tsunami 30 metres high and travelling at several hundred kilometres an hour caused by an underwater earthquake in the Pacific Ocean drowned 26,000 people.

1906   San Francisco, USA: most of the city was destroyed by fire which followed the earthquake.

1923   Tokyo, Japan: probably the most destructive earthquake in modern times, measuring 8.3 on the Richter scale. In this heavily populated city, 140,000 people were killed and more than 575,000 homes were destroyed. The damage caused was estimated to over £1 billion.

1960   Concepcíon, Chile: the most violent earthquake in modern times, which measured 8.5 on the Richter scale and killed more than 5,700 people.

1976   Tangshan, China: the earthquake which probably caused the greatest loss of human life in modern times. It measured 7.8 on the Richter scale and resulted in at least 240,000 deaths, although some estimates put the death-toll as high as 500,000, many of them as a result of famine and disease which followed.

1988   Spitak, Armenia: 55,000 people were killed and 500,000 people made homeless.

The great earthquake of 1907

This story of a terrifying earthquake in Jamaica is told by Gran'Pa in the book, Earthquake, *by Andrew Salkey.*

It happened some time around three-thirty Monday afternoon, the fourteenth of January, two weeks to the day after New Year's Day. I was thirteen at the time. Fourteen in a couple of months. I remember I was at home. It was an ordinary sort of day. Maybe it was a little hotter than usual. But there weren't any signs of disaster anywhere. The sky was blue all over. Mind you, things didn't stay that way for long. At about lunchtime, or some minutes after, a breeze came in off the harbour. We always had a breeze, starting at about ten o'clock in the morning, the "Doctor" breeze, you know. We still call it that. But this twelve o'clock one was different. It was stronger than the "Doctor" and not so cool either. Anyway, it lasted a long time, from twelve or thereabouts until about three o'clock. It was a funny sort of wind, because it made everything feel warmer and boxed in, if you know what I mean, very close and sticky. Yet, in our house on Princess Street, we could see our calico curtains moving in and out of the windows and billowing away, and we could hear the front and back doors banging and clattering about, until we shut them, and the same with our old-fashioned shuttered blinds which were being slammed against the boarding-up of the house. We all started to take notice of the wind in the midst of the heat. It was too obvious to ignore it any longer. And besides, it had brought with it a stillness which was strange for the time of day. Even though the wind was worrying us, there was also a tense feeling hanging over everything, which was frightening. On top of that, there was a street prophet, a man called Turner, who was shouting out things like: "Death and destruction! Run for your lives. Leave Kingston. Judgement is at hand. Leave the wicked now and go up to the hills."

I remember my mother and some of our neighbours talking about Turner. They said he was a madman, a sort of harmless lunatic, roaming the streets and quoting the Bible, but not really causing anybody any harm.

I remembered how they looked too. My mother and the women she was talking to were sweating and chatting to one another without listening or waiting for the replies to what they were saying and they were moving about aimlessly without going anywhere in particular.

And then, at about three o'clock, we all noticed that the wind had dropped away to nothing. By three-thirty, just before it happened, there wasn't a trace anywhere. The whole of our house was dead still. So was our street. I suppose the entire city was silent but for a few sounds. We could still hear some of the usual noises, every now and then. We heard the clanging grinding of the tram-cars and the clip-clop of the horse-drawn buggies. But we didn't hear Turner any more. In any case, we were all certain that something dreadful was definitely going to happen, but we weren't certain what it was going to be.

My mother, my two aunts, my brother, my two sisters and I were sitting in my mother's bedroom. My father was at work on the waterfront. I remember we felt the earth shake slightly at first. Then we heard a roaring sound which began softly, distantly muffled, and suddenly became louder and louder. It sounded like a giant engine, buried in the ground, revving up to get loose and trying to break through and blast its way to the surface. Then we felt a mixture of movements all at once. Our house shook violently and the movements continued, mixing and over-lapping, jarring, bumping, swelling, rumbling, rushing and rocking.

I heard a splitting sound and I saw two of the bedroom walls collapsing and moving towards each other. In a second, they had crashed down and crushed my two aunts and my two sisters. My mother had her arms around me and my brother. Her face was smeared with grit and grime, and her hair was covered with tiny bits of mortar. A heavy, stifling dust filled the room, choking us and blinding us. But even through all that, I could hear the creaking and wrenching of wood and the bending and straining of metal all round me, together with a heavy, thumping vibration.

Suddenly, all three of us, my mother, my brother and I realized exactly what was going on, and my mother started praying, while still holding on to us and moving towards the door. As soon as we got to the entrance, the floor dropped away and the ceiling caved in immediately afterwards, and the only thing left was the lintel of the door under which we were standing huddled together.

Through the swirling dust, I could see that the downward path to the steps was slowly breaking in two. We hesitated and watched the steps in front of us splitting right down the middle. We also saw that the back yard had been cracked open wide in one or two places, with other smaller cracks running along them.

By the time we had jumped from the doorway down to the yard, the shaking had stopped. But other terrible things were going on. We saw a street wall which was very thick (I know it was, because I used to play on it), bending and twisting and tumbling down. Before it fell, I saw several cracks on it, crossing one another and criss-crossing off in many directions.

My mother was still praying and holding on to us. We walked through our back gate and into a lane which would take us back to Princess Street. When we got there, we saw people we knew running wild and hopping over the wide gashes in the street. We heard them crying and cursing from their injuries. We heard shouts coming from under a high mound of rubble.

In one place, farther up Princess Street, after we had heard similar shouts coming from a heap of stone and iron fencing and we were looking at the spot, we saw a complete side of a building collapse on top of it, and the shouts stopped. We had to pick our path in and around the fallen verandas, bricks, mortar and woodwork lying everywhere. And, of course, houses, shop frontages, pillars were still falling, long after the quake. They came crashing down in a sort of weird, sloping slow-motion, with a loud, vibrating bang when they slammed into the ground.

Ruins were everywhere. All the streets and lanes crossing Princess Street east and west were cracked and heaped with rubble. And on our slow, wandering journey there was a thick fog of grit and mortar dust every inch of the way. And worst of all, there were many mysterious outbreaks of fire. In fact, far behind us, beginning at the Victoria Pier and spreading out on either side of King Street, up to the Kingston church, there was a vast burning area.

The people who were straggling through the streets were stumbling about like blind cripples, coughing and spluttering, and crying out in anguish. My mother didn't really know where she was going. I certainly didn't. And my brother was the same. At one stage, I thought we might have been going down to the waterfront to look for Papa, but no. My mother was just walking away from our street and going nowhere in particular.

And that was how we were able to see the things we saw for the first time in our lives. Some of them: a four-poster bed up-ended at a street corner, a smashed piano leaning against an uprooted tree. And we saw a group of survivors levering the broken portions of a building and holding them up with long strips of wood and rafters while a few trapped people crawled out. And we saw others working with bleeding hands to free their relatives and friends from the crushing weight of brick walls and zinc roofs.

When we got to the Race Course, my mother stopped just outside and for the first time since we had left our house, she spoke to us. She squeezed my shoulder and said, "You know that your Aunt Maud and Aunt Edith and your sisters are dead?" She was right, I regret to say, because my father found them later on.

So my mother gave us a gentle push and we jumped over a narrow bed of cannas and we were in the Race Course. It was crowded with people who were camping out all over the place. And as far as I could see, all the open spaces on the way to the Race Course, the small private gardens, the Victoria Park, the roadside benches, were packed with people who had left their houses and walked away in distress and confusion. And to think, all of this had been caused by an earthquake that had lasted no more than between fifteen and twenty seconds.

Pompeii

It was hot, unnaturally hot for a summer's dawn. A violent tremor shook the burning air, followed by a clap of thunder.

The people of Pompeii watched, horrified, as Mount Vesuvius burst open before their very eyes.

White-hot stones hailed down upon the town. Then came the ash, blinding them, choking their mouths and lungs.

Some took cover in the farthest corners of their homes; others tried to escape, fleeing with their families towards the nearby sea.

Very rapidly after 24 August AD 79, judging by the available evidence, Pompeii disappeared completely from the face of the inhabited world. On the level earth, grass and vines gradually took possession of land where the town had once stood. Country people soon forgot even its name, referring to the hill that now covered it by the blank term la città, "the city".

Pliny the Younger was a friend of the Emperor Trajan (AD 97–117), He lived at Misenum, close to Pompeii. In AD 104 he wrote two letters to the historian Tacitus in which he described his memories of the eruption that destroyed Pompeii.

My uncle was stationed at Misenum in active command of the fleet. The ninth day before the Calends of September [24 August], in the early afternoon, my mother drew to his attention a cloud of unusual size and appearance. He had been out in the sun, had taken a cold bath, eaten a light lunch while lying down, and was then working at his books. He called for his shoes and climbed up to a place that would give him the best view of the phenomenon. It was not clear at that distance from which mountain the cloud was rising (it was afterwards known to be Vesuvius). Its general appearance can best be expressed as being like an umbrella pine, for it rose to a great height on a sort of trunk and then split off into branches, I imagine because it was thrust upwards by the first blast and then left unsupported as the pressure subsided, or else it was borne down by its own weight so that it spread out

and gradually dispersed. In places it looked white, elsewhere blotched and dirty, according to the amount of soil and ashes it carried with it. My uncle's scholarly acumen saw at once that it was important enough for a closer inspection, and he ordered a boat to be made ready, telling me I could come with him if I wished. I replied that I preferred to go on with my studies, and as it happened he had himself given me some writing to do.

[*Pliny goes on to describe the rest of his uncle's journey and subsequent death while trying to escape the ash falling from the volcano.*]

You tell me that the letter in which, at your request, I described the death of my uncle has made you want to know what fears and even what dangers I myself experienced, having been left behind in Misenum (in fact, I had reached this point when I interrupted myself). Although I tremble at the very memory, I will begin.

After my uncle's departure, I gave the rest of the day to study – the object which had kept me at home. Afterward I bathed, dined and retired to short and broken sleep. For several days we had experienced earth shocks, which hardly alarmed us as they are frequent in Campania. But that night they became so violent that it seemed the world was not only being shaken, but turned upside down. My mother rushed to my bedroom – I was just rising, as I intended to wake her if she was asleep. We sat down in the courtyard of the house, which separated it by a short distance from the sea. Whether from courage or inexperience (I was eighteen at the time), I called for a volume of Titus Livius and began to read, and even continued my notations from it, as if nothing were the matter. At this moment a friend of my uncle's arrived; he had just returned from Spain to see him. When he saw me sitting there, with my mother, when he saw me reading, he criticised me for my passivity and lack of concern; I continued to pay just as much enthusiastic attention to my book.

Though it was the first hour of the day, the light appeared to us still faint and uncertain. And though we were in an open place, it was narrow, and the buildings around us were so unsettled that the collapse of walls seemed a certainty. We decided to get out of town to escape this menace. The panic-stricken crowds followed us, in response to that instinct of fear which causes people to follow where others lead. In a long close tide they harassed and jostled us. When we were clear of the houses, we stopped, as we encountered fresh prodigies and terrors. Though our carts were on level ground, they were tossed about in every direction, and even when weighted with stones could not be kept steady. The sea appeared to have shrunk, as if withdrawn by the tremors of the earth. In any event, the shore had widened, and many sea-

creatures were beached on the sand. In the other direction loomed a horrible black cloud ripped by sudden bursts of fire, writhing snakelike and revealing sudden flashes larger than lightning.

Then my uncle's friend from Spain began to argue with great energy and urgency. "If your brother," he said, "if your uncle is alive, he would want you to be saved; if he has perished, he would have wanted you to survive. Why, then, do you delay your escape?" We replied that we could not think of our own safety before finding out what had happened to him. Without a moment's further delay, he left us abruptly and escaped the danger in a frantic headlong rush. Soon after, the cloud began to descend upon the earth and cover the sea. It had already surrounded and obscured Capreae (Capri), and blotted out Cape Misenum. My mother now began to beg, urge and command me to escape as best I could. A young man could do it; she, burdened with age and corpulence, would die easy if only she had not caused my

death. I replied that I would not be saved without her. Taking
her hand, I hurried her along. She complied reluctantly, and
not without self-reproach for hindering me.

And now came the ashes, but at first sparsely. I turned
around. Behind us, an ominous thick smoke, spreading over
the earth like a flood, followed us. "Let's go into the fields
while we can still see the way," I told my mother – for I was
afraid that we might be crushed by the mob on the road in
the midst of darkness. We had scarcely agreed when we were
enveloped in night – not a moonless night or one dimmed by
cloud, but the darkness of a sealed room without lights. To be
heard were only the shrill cries of women, the wailing of
children, the shouting of men. Some were calling to their
parents, others to their children, others to their wives –
knowing one another only by voice. Some wept for
themselves, others for their relations. There were those who,
in their very fear of death, invoked it. Many lifted up their
hands to the gods, but a great number believed there were no

gods, and that this was to be the world's last, eternal night. Some added to the real danger with false or illusory terrors: "In Misenum," they would say, "such and such a building has collapsed, and some other is in flames." This might not be true, but it was believed.

A curious brightness revealed itself to us not as daylight but as approaching fire; but it stopped some distance from us. Once more, darkness and ashes, thick and heavy. From time to time we had to get up and shake them off for fear of being actually buried and crushed under their weight. I can boast that in so great a danger, I did not utter a single word or a single lamentation that could have been construed as weakness. I believed that one and all of us would perish – a wretched but strong consolation in my dying. But the darkness lightened, and then like smoke or cloud dissolved away. Finally a genuine daylight came; the sun shone, but pallidly, as in an eclipse. And then, before our terror-stricken gaze everything appeared changed – covered by a thick layer of ashes like an abundant snowfall.

We returned to Misenum, where we refreshed ourselves as best we could. We passed an anxious night between hope and fear – though chiefly the latter, for the earthquakes continued, and some pessimistic people were giving a ghoulish turn to their own and their neighbours' calamities by horrifying predictions. Even so, my mother and I – despite the danger we had experienced and the danger which still threatened – had no thought of leaving until we should receive some word of my uncle.

Such were the events; and you will read about them without the slightest intention of including the information in your works, as they are unworthy of history... Adieu!

34

Pompeii *24 August AD 79*

The giants are sleeping now
under a hot land
where the grey snow
has yet to fall
and cover all
with its dying dew.

The city is silent now
under a haze of blue
till the pedlar's car
on the stone-clad street
calls the early few
for pot or shoe
and the slave from sleep.

The hillside is sunwashed now
where the lush vine
and the olives line
the summer slopes
of the giants' home
in an August dream
that has almost gone.

The gods are sleeping now
unaware
by the temple walls
and market stalls
of the city square...
And an ashen cloud
shrouds the breathless crowd
as the grey snow falls.

Judith Nicholls

Hatchet

"So." He almost jumped with the word, spoken aloud. It seemed so out of place, the sound. He tried it again. "So. So. So here I am."

And there it is, he thought. For the first time since the crash his mind started to work, his brain triggered and he began thinking.

Here I am – and where is that?

Where am I?

He pulled himself once more up the bank to the tall tree without branches and sat again with his back against the rough bark. It was hot now, but the sun was high and to his rear and he sat in the shade of the tree in relative comfort. There were things to sort out.

Here I am and that is nowhere. With his mind opened and thoughts happening it all tried to come in with a rush, all of what had occurred and he could not take it. The whole thing turned into a confused jumble that made no sense. So he fought it down and tried to take one thing at a time.

He had been flying north to visit his father for a couple of months, in the summer, and the pilot had had a heart attack and had died, and the plane had crashed somewhere in the Canadian north woods but he did not know how far they had flown or in what direction or where he was...

Slow down, he thought. Slow down more.

My name is Brian Robeson and I am thirteen years old and I am alone in the north woods of Canada.

All right, he thought, that's simple enough.

I was flying to visit my father and the plane crashed and sank in a lake.

There, keep it that way. Short thoughts.

I do not know where I am.

Which doesn't mean much. More to the point, *they* do

not know where I am – *they* meaning anybody who might be wanting to look for me. The searchers.

They would look for him, look for the plane. His father and mother would be frantic. They would tear the world apart to find him. Brian had seen searches on the news, seen films about lost planes. When a plane went down they mounted extensive searches and almost always they found the plane within a day or two. Pilots all filed flight plans – a detailed plan for where and when they were going to fly, with all the courses explained. They would come, they would look for him. The searchers would get government planes and cover both sides of the flight plan filed by the pilot and search until they found him.

Maybe even today. They might come today. This was the second day after the crash. No. Brian frowned. Was it the first day or the second day? They had gone down in the afternoon and he had spent the whole night out cold. So this was the first real day. But they could still come today. They would have started the search immediately when Brian's plane did not arrive.

Yeah, they would probably come today.

Probably come in here with amphibious planes, small bushplanes with floats that could land right here on the lake and pick him up and take him home.

Which home? The father home or the mother home? He stopped the thinking. It didn't matter. Either on to his dad or back to his mother. Either way he would probably be home by late night or early morning, home where he could sit down and eat a large, cheesy, juicy burger with tomatoes and double fries with ketchup and a thick chocolate milkshake.

And there came hunger.

Brian rubbed his stomach. The hunger had been there but something else – fear, pain – had held it down. Now, with the thought of the burger, the emptiness roared at him. He could not believe the hunger, had never felt it this way. The lake water had filled his stomach but left it hungry, and now it demanded food, screamed for food.

And there was, he thought, absolutely nothing to eat. Nothing.

What did they do in films when they got stranded like this? Oh, yes, the hero usually found some kind of plant that he knew was good to eat and that took care of it. Just ate the plant until he was full or used some kind of cute trap to catch an animal and cook it over a slick little fire and pretty soon he had a full eight-course meal.

The trouble, Brian thought, looking round, was that all he could see was grass and brush. There was nothing obvious to eat and apart from about a million birds and the beaver he hadn't seen animals to trap and cook, and even if he got one somehow he didn't have any matches so he couldn't have a fire...

Nothing.

It kept coming back to that. He had nothing.

Well, almost nothing. As a matter of fact, he thought, I don't know what I've got or haven't got. Maybe I should try and figure out just how I stand. It will give me something to do – keep me from thinking of food. Until they come to find me.

Brian had once had an English teacher, a guy named Perpich, who was always talking about being positive, thinking positive, staying on top of things. That's how Perpich had put it – stay positive and stay on top of things. Brian thought of him now – wondered how to stay positive and stay on top of this. All Perpich would say is that I have to get motivated. He was always telling kids to get motivated.

Brian changed position so that he was sitting on his knees. He reached into his pockets and took out everything he had and laid it on the grass in front of him.

It was pitiful enough. A quarter, three dimes, a nickel, and two pennies. A fingernail clipper. A bill-fold with a twenty-dollar bill – "In case you get stranded at the airport in some small town and have to buy food," his mother had said – and some odd pieces of paper.

And on his belt, somehow still here, the hatchet his mother had given him. He had forgotten it and now reached around and took it out and put it in the grass. There was a touch of rust already forming on the cutting edge of the blade and he rubbed it off with his thumb.

That was it.

He frowned. No, wait – if he was going to play the game, might as well play it right. Perpich would tell him to quit messing around. Get motivated. Look at *all* of it, Robeson.

He had on a pair of good tennis shoes, now almost dry. And socks. And jeans and underwear and a thin leather belt and a T-shirt with an anorak so torn it hung on him in tatters.

And a watch. He had a digital watch still on his wrist but it was broken from the crash – the little screen blank – and he took it off and almost threw it away but stopped the hand motion and lay the watch on the grass with the rest of it.

There. That was it.

No, wait. One other thing. Those were all the things he had, but he also had himself. Perpich used to drum that into them – "You are your most valuable asset. Don't forget that. You are the best thing you have."

Brian looked around again. I wish you were here, Perpich. I'm hungry and I'd trade everything I have for a hamburger.

"I'm hungry." He said it aloud. In normal tones at first, then louder and louder until he was yelling it. "I'm hungry, I'm hungry, I'm hungry!"

When he stopped there was sudden silence, not just from him but the clicks and blurps and bird sounds of the forest as well. The noise of his voice had startled everything and it was quiet. He looked around, listened with his mouth open, and realised that in all his life he had never heard silence before. Complete silence. There had always been some sound, some kind of sound.

It lasted only a few seconds, but it was so intense that it seemed to become part of him. Nothing. There was no sound. Then the birds started again, and some kind of buzzing insect, and then a chattering and a cawing, and soon there was the same background of sound.

Which left him still hungry.

Of course, he thought, putting the coins and the rest back in his pocket and the hatchet in his belt – of course if they come tonight or even if they take as long as tomorrow the hunger is no big thing. People have gone for many days without food as long as they've got water. even if they don't come until late tomorrow I'll be all right. Lose a little weight, maybe, but the first hamburger and milkshake and fries will bring it right back.

A mental picture of a hamburger, the way they showed it in the television commercials, thundered into his thoughts. Rich colours, the meat juicy and hot...

He pushed the picture away. So even if they didn't find him until tomorrow, he thought, he would be all right. He had plenty of water, although he wasn't sure if it was good and clean or not.

He sat again by the tree, his back against it. There was a thing bothering him. He wasn't quite sure what it was but it kept chewing at the edge of his thoughts. Something about the plane and the pilot that would change things...

Ah, there it was – the moment when the pilot had his heart attack his right foot had jerked down on the rudder pedal and the plane had slewed sideways. What did that mean? Why did that keep coming into his thinking that way, nudging and pushing?

It means, a voice in his thoughts said, that they might not be coming for you tonight or even tomorrow. When the pilot pushed the rudder pedal the plane had jerked to the side and assumed a new course. Brian could not remember how much it had pulled round, but it wouldn't have had to be much because after that, with the pilot dead, Brian had flown for hour after hour on the new course.

Well away from the flight plan the pilot had filed. Many hours at maybe 160 miles an hour. Even if it was only a little off course, with that speed and time Brian might now be sitting several hundred miles off to the side of the recorded flight plan.

And they would probably search most heavily at first along the flight plan course. They might go out to the side a little, but he could easily be three, four hundred miles to the side. He could not know, could not think of how far he might have flown wrong, because he didn't know the original course and didn't know how much they had pulled sideways.

Quite a bit – that's how he remembered it. Quite a jerk to the side. It pulled his head over sharply when the plane had swung around.

They might not find him for two or three days. He felt his heartbeat increase as the fear started. The thought was there but he fought it down for a time, pushed it away, then it exploded out.

They might not find him for a long time.

And the next thought was there as well, that they might never find him, but that was panic and he fought it down and tried to stay positive. They searched hard when a plane went down, they used many men and planes and they would go to the side, they would know he was off from the flight path, he had talked to the man on the radio, they would somehow know...

It would be all right.

They would find him. Maybe not tomorrow, but soon. Soon. Soon.

They would find him soon.

Gradually, like sloshing oil his thoughts settled back and the panic was gone. Say they didn't come for two days – no, say they didn't come for three days, even push that to four days – he could live with that. He would have to live with that. He didn't want to think of them taking longer. But say four days. He had to do something. He couldn't just sit at the bottom of this tree and stare down at the lake for four days.

And nights. He was in deep woods and didn't have any matches, couldn't make a fire. There were large things in the woods. There were wolves, he thought, and bears – and other things. In the dark he would be in the open here, just sitting at the bottom of a tree.

He looked around suddenly, felt the hair on the back of his neck go up. Things might be looking at him right now, waiting for him – waiting for dark so they could move in and take him.

He fingered the hatchet at his belt. It was the only weapon he had, but it was something.

He had to have some kind of shelter. No, make that more: he had to have some kind of shelter and he had to have something to eat.

He pulled himself to his feet and jerked the back of his shirt down before the mosquitoes could get at it. He had to do something to help himself.

I have to get motivated, he thought, remembering Perpich. Right now I'm all I've got. I have to do something.

Finding your way

Have you ever wondered how you could find your way in the wilderness without a map or compass? It's possible, and people have been doing it successfully for centuries. Some of the techniques used for navigation are very sophisticated, but there are some simple ones that you could try for yourself, using a compass to check your results.

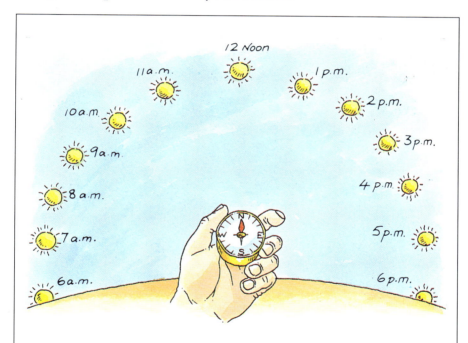

1 If you have a compass but no watch you can still work out the time. When the sun is at its highest point in the sky it is exactly north of you (in the northern hemisphere) or south of you (in the southern hemisphere). The sun reaches its highest point at 12 noon, so when it is directly north of you then you know it is 12 noon. You can use this principle to tell the approximate time of day, whatever the position of the sun.

2   You can find out which way is north using the sun and a stick! Put your stick upright in the ground, and towards midday start measuring the shadow the stick casts by putting a stone at the end of the shadow. Do this every fifteen minutes or so. The shadow will gradually shorten towards noon and lengthen from then on, so the shortest shadow will be cast at noon. The shortest shadow will therefore point north in the northern hemisphere and south in the southern hemisphere.

3   A needle, a bowl of water and a blade of grass can be used as a compass! Magnetise the needle, using a magnet or by brushing it against silk. Float a blade of grass in a bowl of water, then put the needle on top of the grass. It should point in a north-south direction.

4 The stars are a good way of finding direction. In the northern hemisphere, the easiest way to find north is to look for the Plough, which is also called the Great Bear or Big Dipper. Actually, it looks more like a saucepan with a bent handle – look in a book on star constellations and find a picture of it. The two stars which make up the side of the saucepan opposite the handle point towards the North Star (also called the Pole Star), which shows the exact position of the North Pole. In the southern hemisphere you need to look for the Southern Cross. The two stars that make up the longest axis of the cross point south – not exactly, but near enough to go by.

5 Most people know that you can tell the age of a tree by the rings in the tree stump, but it's a little known fact that the rings will be wider apart on the north (in the northern hemisphere) or south (in the southern hemisphere).

6 Trees and shrubs standing on their own are affected by wind and sun. So if you know which way the prevailing winds blow in the area you are in, for example south–west, the wind will have swept the branches of single trees and shrubs towards the north-east. More moss will grow on the side of the tree trunk which receives the least sunlight.

7 Other plants and animals make good direction indicators. If you're in southern Africa, you can find north using the North Pole plant, which is named after the direction it leans towards. The African weaver bird only ever builds its nest on the west side of trees.

Did you know that there are actually three "norths"? True north is the position of the earth's geographical North Pole, magnetic north is the direction your compass points, and grid north is the north marked on maps. In most parts of the world, these three points are similar enough to make very little difference. But there are some places where the three are quite different. This is called "magnetic variation" and is marked on most maps, so that anyone travelling in that area can adjust their compass reading accordingly.

Monsoon

Where do the fish go
When the monsoon
Thunders on the water
And the foam churns
Like milk?

Where do the birds hide
When the trees fall
In high winds
And all the fruit
Lies everywhere
On field and ground?

Where do people run
When the rain comes through
The thatch?
And the floods creep in on them
Like thieves?

Alfreda de Silva

If a shark attacks...

There is generally no reason to fear shark attacks if you are sensible. The following rules will make sure you are unlikely to be one of the 100 people around the world who are attacked every year. Some advice is obvious, some common sense, and some very difficult to follow if you suddenly come face to face with a great white shark. It is easy to say "Don't panic!" – but probably much harder to do!

1. Don't swim in areas where sharks have been sighted.

2. Don't swim at night – that's the time when sharks prefer to feed.

3. If you spot a shark get out of the water as quickly and quietly as you can. Splashes and loud noises attract sharks – so swim smoothly.

4. Don't swim alone in risky waters. Have someone as a lookout.

5. Don't wear contrasting colours – for example black and white. Sharks can't see colours, but they can see sharp contrasts.

6. Don't wear jewellery – flashing metal attracts sharks.

7. If you can't get out of the water, then keep the shark in view – sharks rarely attack humans who are facing them.

8. Leave the water if you have even the slightest cut – sharks' powerful ability to scent blood will attract them from a kilometre away.

9. If you've been fishing then remember that the blood of the fish you catch could also attract a shark.

10. If everything else fails, then scream at the shark (it sometimes scares them off) or punch it on the snout.

Shark defences

Over the centuries many people have tried to come up with a defence against sharks. Some have been more successful than others...

I Stripy suits — 0/10

Sharks are supposed to be afraid of banded sea snakes. So, dress a swimmer in a wet suit that has black and white hoops around it and the shark will swim off in terror.

Does it work? As sharks are attracted to contrasting colours, it's not surprising that an experienced diver said it had absolutely no effect at all.

2 Shark armour — 5/10

Metal suits made of a sort of chain-mail will stop small sharks from tearing lumps of flesh from a swimmer. It has worked in tests with 2-metre sharks. However a large shark would still almost certainly do some serious damage with the sheer power of its jaws. Anyway, it could carry off the diver (and the suit) in one piece.

3 Shark nets   5/10

Placing a net across part of a bay makes it safer for swimmers. The success can be seen in the number of sharks caught each year. They have been tried in Sydney (1937) with fair success. But on one South African beach the shark attacks increased after nets were tried!

4 Spear guns   1/10

By themselves spear guns don't work too well. The shark has to be struck in the brain – and that's a very small target. Sharks can be stabbed many times in the body and will still keep attacking.

5 Powerheads   6/10

Attach an explosive charge to a spear gun and you have a much more useful weapon. They still require the diver to be an accurate shot, however.

6 Gas injection darts 4/10

These are another device attached to a spear gun. The dart sticks into the shark and fills it with carbon dioxide gas, so that it blows up like a balloon. When it floats to the surface it quickly suffocates. But to do this, the diver has to hit the body from the side or from below. Head-on shots don't work – and if a shark is attacking it will come at you head on.

7 Electric shark repellents 7/10

Built into a wet suit, electric shark repellents will give the shark a shock if it so much as touches a diver. They work, but they're so expensive they have not been used very much.

8 Shark screen 8/10

A sort of life belt with a bag hanging under it. Once a swimmer is in the bag s/he becomes invisible to a shark. Very useful for crashed aeroplane passengers or sunken boat survivors. Obviously no use to a sport/fun swimmer.

9   Shark chasers 0/10

Chemicals which a shark scents, dislikes and swims away from. Various types have been tested. All claim to make a swimmer completely safe. In fact, none of them work.

10   Bubble barrier 0/10

The theory was that bubbles from divers' gas bottles drove off sharks. There were many experiments with barriers of bubbles. The plan was that humans could swim behind a bubble curtain, while sharks would be turned away. Great idea. Unfortunately they don't seem to work.

The Eyam woman

Memory can play tricks. A story can become twisted as people remember the unusual or the heroic. They forget the other side of the story. They forget that, in a disaster, some people never change. While a disaster brings out courage, it can also bring out greed, cowardice and cruelty. The people of Eyam are remembered for their goodness during the 1665–66 plague. But it wasn't quite that simple...

Eyam village, Derbyshire – 1666

They call me "The Eyam woman" now. They look at me with suspicion. Children run away screaming when they see me in the street. Even older people keep as far away as they can when they pass me by. It's as if I'm a leper. I'm not. It's all because of what happened in Eyam back in 1666.

You probably know the story. It's famous. If you don't I'll repeat it for you ... but I'll tell you the truth.

Eyam is a village up in the hills of Derbyshire. It's a dozen miles or so from the nearest large town. The middle of nowhere, you might say. But the lead mines brought work for the men and a village grew around that work. It's a village like ten thousand others. But Eyam became famous.

Of course the people of Eyam had heard of plagues in London. They say the city's dirty and dangerous. If the cut-throats and the footpads and the kidnappers don't get you, then the sickness will.

The last great sickness was in 1665. We had word of it – thousands dying every week – but we felt safe in our little village in the clean air of the hills. Maybe we were proud. Maybe that pride brought the plague as a punishment. Some of the women thought it was some other sin that made God angry. In the springtime some village boys had chased cattle into the church – the cattle left their droppings on the floor. The plague was sent as a punishment for that, they said. The boys are dead now, of course.

Some people said they saw the spirits of dead children flying over the village. Others saw white crickets sitting in their hearths. Sure signs of disaster. I saw nothing. Our farm stood on the hillside above the village. The first I knew of the disaster was when I went to church one September Sunday back in 1665 and the Rector, William Mompesson, climbed up to the pulpit with a worried face.

Mr Mompesson was a young man. He'd only been with us a year, but he had a lot of help from the old Rector, Thomas Stanley. Of course people forget Mr Stanley when they're talking about the heroes of Eyam. It's always Mr Mompesson they think of.

That Sunday Mr Mompesson spoke in a slow, serious voice. "My friends," he said, "This week our village has been visited by a pestilence. Widow Cooper had taken in a tailor as her lodger. Some of you may have met him. His name was George Viccars. Mr Viccars had begun to sell clothes in Eyam and needed some more cloth. It seems a parcel was delivered from London some two weeks ago. You know about the plague in London. It is probable that this cloth contained the infection."

My children grew restless beside me. "What's a plague, mamma?" Elizabeth asked me.

"Hush! Listen to the Rector," I said.

He went on, "George Viccars died. We mourned him and buried him. I am only sorry there was no money to buy a headstone for his grave. But in the past two weeks there have been six more plague victims. They were all neighbours of Mr Viccars. We thought we had buried the plague with the tailor... it seems we were mistaken. I know that many of you are afraid. I can only tell you to put your faith in the Lord and pray."

During prayers I looked around the church. There were six empty seats where the plague victims used to sit. But there were more than just those six. At the end of the service I asked Beth Hancock, "Where are the Bradshaw family?"

She gathered her children round her and whispered. "They've left the village. Run away. I wish we could do the same."

"They are rich," I said. "They can afford to leave and set up a new home. We are tied to the farm. If we left it we'd starve."

"Aye," Beth Hancock said bitterly. "And if you don't leave it you risk the plague. The Lord punishes the sinners of Eyam – but not the rich sinners."

We returned to the farm, my husband John, me and the six children. I tried to tell them that the plague was just a sickness; I told them not to worry ... that if they were good children they wouldn't catch it. My lies may have protected the children from the fear. It could not protect them from the sickness in the end.

As the winter grew colder the disease became weaker. Eighty people died before Easter of 1666. That was sad enough. Old friends; families we'd sold eggs and milk to; children that my family had known since they were born. All dead before Easter. How do you explain to your son that he'll never see his friend again this side of Judgement Day?

The thing that kept us going was knowing that it could have been worse.

In London the plague was finished. People began to return to the capital. In Eyam that May only four people died. The Bradshaws hadn't returned but the rest of us began to live life as normal.

Then, just as we were sure we were safe from the clutches

of Death, he returned. For Death doesn't die. That May he had only been sleeping a little while.

In June, Death breathed and blew away the people of Eyam like dandelion seeds in a gale. There was no resisting him. No herbs, no potions, no prayers, no charms could stop him. He swept away families and emptied houses. John and I thought of sending the children to my brother in Sheffield. But there were six of them. It was too much to ask.

Rector Mompesson's wife begged him to take her and their two children away. He said they could go without him, but he had to stay. In the end his wife Catherine stayed, but their children went. Don't ever forget that. In the dreadful six months that followed, Mompesson's children were safe in Doncaster.

That is when Rector Mompesson came up with the scheme that made him a hero in the land. First he closed the church. We believed that standing closer than three paces to a plague victim could infect you. Victims carried the bad air with them. It would be foolish to bring the sick and the well together in the church.

He told us all to meet at a spot called Cucklett Delph, a sheltered hollow with a stream running through it. We stood in family groups, not daring to come too close to other families. Rector Mompesson climbed onto a rock and told us what he wanted us to do. "The village of Eyam has been visited by the plague," he said. "We have faced it bravely until now and borne our sufferings with courage. However, we have a duty to others outside of our village. We cannot risk carrying this dreadful infection to other towns. I would ask you to stay in the village for however long it takes. Do not leave Eyam while there is the chance that you might carry the plague with you."

It was to be a death sentence for many of the people gathered in Cucklett Delph. "How will we eat?" my husband asked. "Eyam does not produce enough of its own food. We need to get to market."

The Rector nodded. "The Earl of Devonshire who owns much of our land has offered to provide for us. If there is anything else we need then it can be left at the village boundary. We can leave the money at the boundary marker stone. I have had a hollow carved in the stone. It will be filled with vinegar. We will leave money in the vinegar so the collector will not catch the disease."

"What if we choose to leave?" someone asked.

"Then there are guards on the road. You will be brought back." He looked around the silent crowd and said,

"Remember, our Lord died so others might live. We in Eyam can do no less. Any one person leaving will betray the rest of the village."

I'll swear he was looking at me when he said that. Perhaps it was my conscience – escape was exactly what I had been thinking of.

"I have one more thing to say," Rector Mompesson announced. "We have lost two grave-diggers and the church can no longer help you to bury your dead. Each family must in future bury their own dead. In their gardens, in the orchards or in the fields. There will be no church services for them, but Rector Stanley and I will say prayers. Each Sunday we will hold the usual services, but we will hold them here. May God be with you," he finished, and left us to walk the lonely path back to our farm. Our prison.

I went with the children each day to the village with eggs and milk for sale. I exchanged news with the other women.

We talked about the latest victims ... and every time the talk came around to escape. "I would kill anyone who tried to flee from Eyam," Sarah Carter said. Again I felt the shame of my own guilty thoughts and turned away.

I do not want to tell of August 1666, but I suppose I must. Seventy people and seven died in that dreadful month. I'm sorry, I cannot care about the seventy. I can only care about the seven. My seven.

The children grew bored on the farm and went into the village to play. Those they played with died within a week. After two weeks my son Edward complained of a fever. He sneezed. A red rash appeared on his skin. Purple lumps swelled painfully under his arms. He died. But even while my husband buried him, William, Alice and Anne fell sick. On 7th August my husband buried all three in shallow graves in the field below the house. Elizabeth followed two days later. Henry and Charles followed on 10th August.

I had cried when the first of my children died. I had no tears left for the last. My husband and I had the fever on 12th August. I lay down and waited to die. I welcomed Death like an old friend who would unite me with my children. I fell asleep that night and hoped I'd never wake in this life.

But I did. As my husband breathed his last breath the next morning I grew stronger every minute. Some people did get better in Eyam that summer – and those who did were safe from ever catching the plague again.

I was one of the unlucky ones who lived.

I wandered into the village hardly knowing where I was going, or why. That was when I met Marshall Howe, a foul-smelling, grey-skinned miner.

"Good day, Mrs Taylor," he said. "How are the family?"

"Dead, Mr Howe, all dead."

"Sorry to hear that, Mrs Taylor. If you need any help, just let me know."

"Help?"

"Burying your loved ones. I've set up in business as a grave-digger. I only charge a sovereign a grave," he said.

"My husband ..." I said.

"You want him burying?" he asked with a strange and ghoulish joy.

What could I do? I led the way back up the hill and he chatted happily. "Terrible times, Mrs Taylor," he said. "My wife and son have just died. Still, life must go on."

"Why?" I asked.

He chuckled and said, "It's a busy time for me. To keep up with the work I'm digging graves while the sick are still breathing. Hah! The other day I almost buried one while he was alive! James Unwin, my neighbour, in fact. He was almost gone so I dug his grave and went to collect him. Tied a bedsheet round his ankles and dragged him out of the door. He suddenly sat up and asked for water! Just in time! He's getting better now!" The man laughed. I felt sickened ... but not by the plague. He talked on.

"Have you heard about Margaret Blackwell? She fell ill last week and her brother had no hope for her. He cooked himself some bacon for breakfast and poured the fat into a jug before he left for work. Poor Margaret woke up with a feverish thirst and grabbed the jug of warm fat. She drank it back, thinking it was milk. It made her sick, of course, but the miracle was it cured her! I've been trying to sell that bacon-fat idea as a plague cure myself. Well, a man has to make a living, doesn't he?"

I didn't answer. We reached the farm and I left him to bury my John. He came to the door half an hour later for his money. "For another sovereign I'll make sure you are buried when your turn comes," he said.

I closed the door on him. The house was quiet. No more sighing and crying of the sick. Only the ghosts of my family. So many, so short a time.

I couldn't milk the cows and herd the sheep and cut the hay all by myself! I needed help. I'll swear that was all that was on my mind when I walked out.

I didn't go by the road. I went over the hills and reached Tideswell later that afternoon. There were guards on the road to the town. "Where are you from?" the man asked.

"Orchard Bank," I said, and that was true. It was the place where I'd buried my family.

"Where's that?" he asked.

"In the land of the living," I said and walked past him.

It was when I asked a woman the road to Sheffield that she looked at me closely – and screamed. She'd recognised me. We'd sold our lambs to her at Tideswell market. "Eyam woman!" she shouted. "Eyam woman!"

In moments I was in the centre of a swirling mass of hatred. People threw vegetables, sticks, mud and stones at me till I was driven all the way back to Eyam.

Their hatred was bad enough. The hatred of the Eyam villagers was worse. I was the traitor who had let them down. I was the one who did what they only dreamed of doing and escaped.

When winter came the plague finally left Eyam. At last they opened the roads and I went to stay with my brother. I'm there now.

The Rector Mompesson became a hero. His wife died of the plague ... and I'm truly sorry for that ... but his children lived. Mine didn't.

Even the vile Marshall Howe is respected in his village. I am despised wherever I go.

I am "The Eyam woman". I am the traitor. I am the unforgiven.

Why?

The fire of London

The plague had come to Eyam from London. It was eradicated there in 1666 by the Great Fire of London, which destroyed the city in just a few days. Samuel Pepys lived in London at the time and described his experience of the fire in his diary. Pepys's diary is now world famous.

September 2nd 1666

Some of our mayds sitting up late last night to get things ready against our feast to-day, Jane called us up about three in the morning to tell us of a great fire they saw in the City. So I rose and slipped on my night-gown and went to her window, and thought it to be on the back-side of Marke-lane at the farthest; but, being unused to such fires as followed, I thought it far enough off; and so went to bed again and to sleep. About seven rose again to dress myself, and there looked out at the window and saw the fire not so much as it

was, and further off. So to my closett to set things to rights
after yesterday's cleaning. By and by Jane comes and tells me
that she hears that above 300 houses have been burned down
to-night by the fire we saw, and that it is now burning down
all Fish-street, by London Bridge. So I made myself ready
presently and walked to the Tower, and there got up upon
one of the high places, Sir J. Robinson's little son going up
with me; and there I did see the houses at that end of the
bridge all on fire, and an infinite great fire on this and the
other side the end of the bridge. So with my heart full of
trouble, I down to the water-side, and there got a boat and
through bridge, and there saw a lamentable fire. Poor
Michell's house, as far as the Old Swan, already burned that
way, and the fire running further. Everybody endeavouring to
remove their goods, and flinging into the river or bringing
them into lighters that lay off; poor people staying in their
houses as long as till the very fire touched them, and then
running into boats, or clambering from one pair of stairs by
the water-side to another. And among other things the poor
pigeons, I perceive, were loth to leave their houses, but
hovered about the windows and balconys till they were, some
of them burned, their wings, and fell down. Having staid, and
in an hour's time seen the fire rage every way, and nobody, to
my sight, endeavouring to quench it, but to remove their
goods and leave all to the fire; and having seen it get as far as
the Steele-yard, and the wind mighty high and driving it into
the City, and every thing after so long a drought proving
combustible, even the very stones of the churches, I to White
Hall and there up to the King's closett in the Chappell, where
people come about me and I did give them an account
dismayed them all, and word was carried in to the King. So I
was called for and did tell the King and Duke of Yorke what

I saw, and that unless his Majesty did command houses to be pulled down nothing could stop the fire. They seemed much troubled, and the King commanded me to go to my Lord Mayor from him and command him to spare no houses, but to pull down before the fire every way. At last met my Lord Mayor in Canning-street like a man spent, with a handkercher about his neck. To the King's message he cried, like a fainting woman, "Lord! what can I do? I am spent: people will not obey me. I have been pulling down houses, but the fire overtakes us faster than we can do it." That he needed no more soldiers; and that, for himself, he must go and refresh himself, having been up all night. So he left me, and I him, and walked home, seeing people all almost distracted; and no manner of means used to quench the fire.

Having seen as much as I could now, I away to White Hall by appointment, and there walked to St. James's Parke, and there met my wife and Creed, and walked to my boat;

and there upon the water again, and to the fire up and down, it still encreasing, and the wind great. So near the fire as we could for smoke; and all over the Thames, with one's face in the wind, you were almost burned with a shower of fire-drops. This is very true; so as houses were burned by these drops and flakes of fire, three or four, nay five or six houses, one from another. When we could endure no more upon the water, we to a little ale-house on the Bankside, over against the Three Cranes, and there staid till it was dark almost, and saw the fire grow; and, as it grew darker, appeared more and more, and in corners and upon steeples, and between churches and houses as far as we could see up the hill of the City, in a most horrid malicious bloody flame, not like the fine flame of an ordinary fire. We staid till, it being darkish, we saw the fire as only one entire arch of fire from this to the other side the bridge, and in a bow up the hill for an arch of above a mile long: it made me weep to see it. The churches, houses and all on fire and flaming at once; and a horrid noise the flames made, and the cracking of houses at their ruine. So home with a sad heart, and there find poor Tom Hater come with some few of his goods saved out of his house, which is burned. I invited him to lie at my house and did receive his goods but was deceived in his lying there, the newes coming every moment of the growth of the fire; so as we were forced to begin to pack up our owne goods and prepare for their removal; and did by moonshine (it being brave dry and moonshine and warm weather) carry much of my goods into the garden, and Mr Hater and I did remove my money and iron chests into my cellar, as thinking that the safest place. And got my bags of gold into my office ready to carry away, and my chief papers of accounts also there, and my tallys into a box by themselves.

James Scott – the ice man

When searchers found James Scott, huddled in an ice cave in Nepal, he had lost twenty-five kilograms in weight and couldn't feel his feet. His kidneys had shut down and his vision and balance had been affected.

James had been lost in the Himalayas for forty-three days, in temperatures that often fell below zero. Doctors and mountain experts were amazed that James had survived. They said it was a miracle he hadn't died in the mountains.

Late in 1991, James Scott, a twenty-two-year-old medical student from the University of Queensland, travelled to Kathmandu in Nepal, to gain experience working in an overseas hospital.

James wanted to do some walking in the Himalayas. He left on a five-day trek, expecting to be back in Kathmandu by Christmas Eve. On 22 December, James and another trekker aimed to cross a high altitude pass. When a snowstorm blew up, James decided to leave his companion and turn back. However, snow had covered the trail and James wandered, lost, for four days before finding shelter under a rock overhang. All he had left to eat were two chocolate bars.

When James was reported missing, his sister, Mrs Joanne Robertson, flew to Kathmandu. Joanne was very determined that James would be found. She co-ordinated the search, and persuaded officials to keep it going long after mountain experts were sure James must be dead.

Joanne refused to accept this and she was right. James wasn't dead. But, living only on melted snow and his two chocolate bars, he wasn't far from it. He was suffering from cold, malnutrition and dehydration. His body was actually cannibalising itself: after using up his fat reserves it had begun on the muscles themselves.

James said later that every night, as the cold set in, he expected to die. Every morning, he was surprised to find himself still alive.

Days went by. A thousand square kilometres were searched and eventually his family decided that James must be trapped in one of three small areas. On 2 February, a helicopter flew into one of these areas and James managed to crawl out and wave to the rescuers.

Two weeks later, James was back in Australia, under the care of a special medical team. The doctors said his survival was a "miracle".

How had James survived?

James was a medical student. He knew what was happening to his body, and how to minimise the effects of the intense cold and lack of food. He prevented serious frostbite by keeping as dry and warm as he could.

James also held a black belt in karate. His teacher said later that James's training, with its mental and physical discipline, had helped him survive. James himself believed the efforts of his family and fiancée had been the reasons he survived. He said it was – "love, hope, prayers – and a bit of medical knowledge and karate discipline."

Twelve months after his rescue, James Scott was still suffering from fatigue and problems with his vision. Doctors think he could have vision problems for the rest of his life.

But in that twelve months, James had also married, returned to his studies, raised money for charities in Kathmandu and written a book about his experiences.

Among the things James Scott most appreciates now, he says, "are good friends, good meals and a warm bed."

EARTHWEEK:

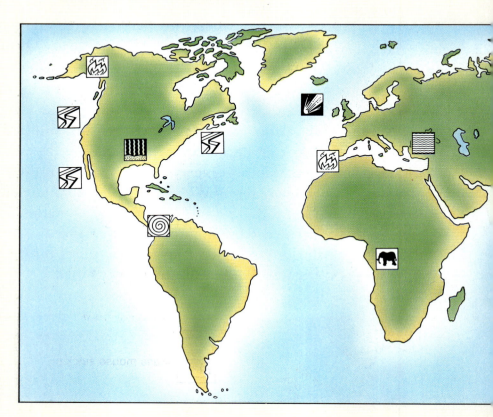

FIERCE FLOODS

 Desperate officials in China's eastern province of Jiangsu blew up a dam on the Xinyi He River to release waters that had ravaged more than 1000 villages and flooded 329,000 acres of cropland in twenty-four Chinese counties. In Shandong Province, fifty-nine miners were trapped underground when water poured into the mine entrance. Major rescue efforts continued through the week.

A DIARY OF THE PLANET

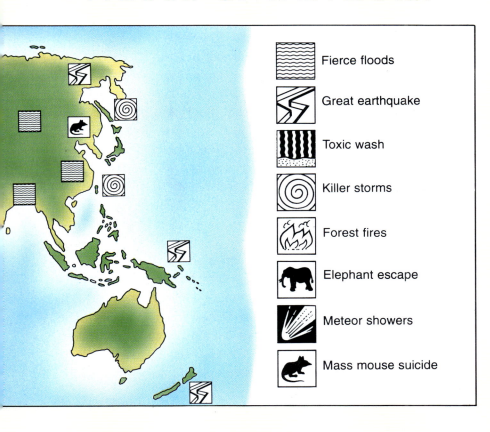

Fierce floods

Great earthquake

Toxic wash

Killer storms

Forest fires

Elephant escape

Meteor showers

Mass mouse suicide

Floods in Russia's Gomei region covered more than 100,000 acres of land near the Chernobyl nuclear plant, destroying roads, bridges and dams. The Selenga River in Russia's Buryatia Republic near Mongolia overflowed, covering dozens of villages and wrecking bridges that connect the capital, Ulan-Ude, with the outside world. Monsoon floods and landslides swept away several villages in India and Nepal. Floodwaters damaged Nepal's largest hydroelectric project, reducing the country's electrical supply by one third.

GREAT EARTHQUAKE

 One of the strongest earthquakes this century rocked the US Pacific island of Guam but caused no deaths. The magnitude 8.1 quake damaged tourist hotels, wrecked bridges, and tossed cars into rivers. Damage forced the Joint Typhoon Warning Center to close while monitoring Typhoon Steve, which struck Guam during the tremor. New Zealand was jolted by two earthquakes that broke water mains, damaged roads and caused power shortages in the city of Gisborne. There were no fatalities. Six people were killed in Nepal by two earthquakes centred in Afghanistan and felt in Russia, Pakistan and India. Earth movements also struck San Francisco, western South Carolina, Alaska and Japan.

TOXIC WASH

 Receding waters of the Mississippi River and its tributaries may contain a "witch's brew" of toxins released by munition dumps, gasoline stations, industrial concerns, and sewage treatment plants. The US Environmental Protection Agency identified twenty-seven flooded hazardous material sites. In Chesterfield, Missouri, dead fish and other waste lying in the streets caused a stench that could be smelled for several miles.

KILLER STORMS

 Tropical storm Bret struck Venezuela, killing 150 people, then causing floods in Costa Rica and Nicaragua. Typhoon Robyn triggered floods and landslides in Japan before moving on to South Korea, where 50,000 ships and boats pulled into port. Robyn then swept north and caused flooding in Vladivostok where eight inches of rain fell in two days.

FOREST FIRES

Bombs left over from the Spanish Civil War detonated as a forest fire burned near Valencia on Spain's east coast. Another blaze in the mountains near Granada threatened the habitat of a rare mountain goat. Other fires burned in the province of Tarragona, southern France, the French Riviera, the island of Corsica, and Italy. A forest fire in Alaska has covered more than 158,000 acres near the community of Circle.

ELEPHANT ESCAPE

Up to one hundred elephants joined thousands of refugees fleeing into Uganda from southern Sudan to escape the civil war. Game wardens guided the herd to safety in Murchison National Park. Elephants also have migrated to escape sporadic ethnic fighting and civil war in Zaire.

METEOR SHOWERS

Poor weather cheated the Netherlands, Ireland, and Britain of a clear view of the Perseid meteor shower. Astronomer and broadcaster Patrick Moore said from his home south of London, "I can't see a thing. It's most annoying. I've all my equipment with me here, but it's very cloudy."

MASS MOUSE SUICIDES

Carcasses of 300,000 mice of a species locally known as "big-eyed devils" were found dead in the waters and on the shore of a lake in China's Fuhai County. A team from the local locust and mouse disaster forecasting station saw large groups of mice plunging into rivers and lakes but could not explain the bizarre behaviour. Alarmed authorities ordered an immediate investigation.

(for the week ending 13 August 1993)

Glossary

acumen insight, understanding

amphibious able to land on or move in water

calico a type of cotton cloth

combustible possible to burn

corpulence large size, obesity

detonated exploded

encreasing old-fashioned spelling of increasing

footpads highway men without horses

gasoline petrol

handkercher handkerchief or scarf

illusory unreal

lamentation cry of mourning or complaint

lintel the bar across the top of a doorway that supports the weight of the wall above

loth reluctant

mayds old-fashioned spelling of maids – girl servants

notations note taking

ominous threatening

pallidly in a pale or weak way

passivity lack of reaction

pestilence infectious disease, plague

phenomenon remarkable event

revelry celebrations

sovereign an old-fashioned gold coin worth £1

spume sea foam

starboard the right-hand side of a ship

tallys detailed accounts

winched reeled in